NECESSARY ENDS

Marvin Cohen

BROADWAY PLAY PUBLISHING INC
New York
www.broadwayplaypub.com
info@broadwayplaypub.com

NECESSARY ENDS
© Copyright 1982 Marvin Cohen

Cover art from the New York Shakespeare Festival production

First published by B P P I in 1985 in *Plays From The New York Shakespeare Festival*

This edition: December 2021
I S B N: 978-0-88145-910-4

Book design: Marie Donovan

An Unnecessary Autobiographical
Pre-beginning to *Necessary Ends*

Necessary Ends was a collaboration with the director James Milton. He suggested many wholesale elaborate changes, scene by scene, from my original shorter version, with the result as published here.

Necessary Ends was privately auditioned to Mr. Papp and his brain staff, with Wallace Shawn, Andre Gregory, Angela Pietropinto, and Gretchen Van Riper in the four roles.

Necessary Ends is still a "virgin" (in case some theater company wants to premiere it), because its run at the Public Theater was a workshop production, with no official "opening" and no invited press reviewers.

Earlier, James Milton had adapted, from two unpublished novels by me, a play, *The Don Juan and the Non-Don Juan*. It was produced in London, but is still a *U.S.* "virgin" (in case some theater company wants to U.S.-premiere it). It had staged readings at the Public Theater, N.Y.U.'s Loeb Student Center, and Los Angeles' Groundlings Theater. Appearing in it at one time or another were Richard Dreyfuss, Keith Carradine, Wallace Shawn, Jill Eikenberry, Lewis J. Stadlen, Mimi Kennedy, Larry Pine, Gretchen Van Riper, and Alma Cuervo.

The newest "virgin" (in case, etc.) is *Topsy-Turvy*, a recent collaboration with the playwright and director Tom Riccio. It's about to be workshopped at the Cleveland Playhouse.

Speaking of Cleveland, I was born and grew up in Brooklyn, the Bensonhurst part. For the last many years, I've been living in Manhattan's Lower East Side. I worked in an odd assortment of different jobs in occupational miscellany. I only got about halfway through college, so no degree. But by being a "published author," I was able to conduct writing workshops, first for college undergraduates at City College (C.C.N.Y.), and then for adult- or continuing-education programs at Queens College, Hofstra, Adelphi, C.W. Post (currently), and the New School (currently).

For a while in the sixties I lived in London. A sort of episodic novel, *The Self-Devoted Friend*, had been rejected by New Directions in New York, but in London a publisher got New Directions to share the production (thus reducing expenses for both houses). The same two ocean-divided houses also published *The Monday Rhetoric of the Love Club, and Other Parables*. Books by other publishers: *Fables at Life's Expense*; *The Inconvenience of Living* (collection of short fictions); *Baseball the Beautiful* (eulogistic essays on philosophy/baseball); *Others, Including Morstive Sternbump* (a novel); and a collection of fictions by Gull Books, *Aesthetics in Life and Art. Existence in Function and Essence. And Whatever Else is Important, too*.

One book, *The Hard Life of a Stone*, has been rejected by publishers on the grounds that the title would render it unsuitable for a paperback edition. My offer to change the title did not soften the publishers' hearts. (Even cardiologists, who call spades spades, wouldn't call those hearts hearts.)

That last paragraph was the only fib of this self-autobiography—I swear on a stack of pancakes.

Currently, I'm being guided by two literary friends in putting together a miscellany cross-section selection sampler of (from a small pile) my book-published pieces, as well as (from a larger pile) my periodical- and anthology-published pieces, and (from the overwhelmingly largest pile) my unpublished pieces: all com-*piled* into a sort of *Marvin Cohen Omnibus*, of unknown route. If any publisher....

Currently, I'm trying to collaborate with a composer (former oboe-ist) in a musical play/opera: My words to his music. Problem is, I can't read music. So he pianos his song music onto a cassette, including abstracting the melody; so then from dummy-lyrics and repeated re-hearings, I arrive at lyrics, from which he criticizes and I revise accordingly. If any impressario would like to risk an adventurous sum of money....

After, as a result of, living in London for a while in the sixties, I've been staying there for a spell of practically every summer since, as an annual visit, mainly extensively social.

I also have a nice social life in New York, flavored and peppered by a helpful sprinkle of parties.

My favorite thing in life is to hit a thrown ball with a bat. I've been doing a little of that in London (cricket), and more in New York/Brooklyn (baseball bat on softball; and broomstick bat on tennis balls in schoolyards).

The dread of no longer being able to connect bat to ball (even in old-age imagination) is behind the play printed in this book, *Necessary Ends*, which is based on the dread of that notoriously bad old life-ender, Death. Death deservedly has been given a bad press, and no wonder.

Other passions of which death is an ugly enemy-in-the-wings are Gilbert and Sullivan, and the human voice in general, especially to Mozart. Also, watching professional football on T.V. My happiest pride of triumph is when the Yankees end a season by winning pennant, League Championship Series, and World Series. Since I identify with them in indissoluble oneness, it's as if I've been elected King of the World.

If I *were* King of the World, I'd aim to alleviate as many human woes and miseries as possible, wherever people live: to lift as many prospects as possible, with the least long-term or short-term cost and damage to others.

I've been trying to figure out life philosophically, meaning what makes people psychologically tick. It has to do with what people want and then their *learning not to want* when such wanting is shown to be of no avail, or no longer of any avail; and their developing new wants that do have more probable hopeful possibilities of getting themselves, by the outside world of mainly people but including one's body itself, co-operated with.

(No piece of writing should ever end with "with." Such an effect of undignified irregularity may well be dispensed with.)

(In order, therefore, not to end this car-biography—I mean auto-biography—with "with," I'll go on:)

Life seems very strange, in that so many people are, and were, living it. As only one of its current practitioners, I'm modestly put in place. I'm numbered, among those numerous current practicners, until my number is up.

Any number can play. But my playing declines, as I get numb-er.

Necessary Ends ran at the Public's Lu Esther Hall from December 12–26, 1982, for a total of 20 performances, under the direction of James Milton, with the following cast:

Georgia	Alma Cuervo
Burt	Larry Pine
Jasper	Bill Sadler
Ginger	Gretchen Van Ryper

The Scenery was constructed by Jim Clayburgh, the Costumes by Amanda J. Klein, the Lighting by John Gisondi, and the Music by Robert Dennis.

Characters

BURT (boyfriend of GEORGIA, friend of JASPER)
GEORGIA (girlfriend of BURT)
JASPER (boyfriend of GINGER, friend of BURT)
GINGER (girlfriend of JASPER)

Time: Now

Place: Optional

> "Of all the wonders that I yet have heard,
> It seems to me most strange that men should fear;
> Seeing that death, a necessary end,
> Will come when it will come."
> > (*Julius Caesar*, Act II, Scene II)

Scene One

(The getting-into-bed ritual of BURT *and* GEORGIA. *This could include (but not necessarily) brushing of teeth, listening to radio, undressing and getting into night clothes, reading, eating, playing cards or a game, etc. Action should establish the practicality and precision of* BURT *and* GEORGIA *(though hers is inorganic, hence she might have a lapse or two). Couple then turn off lamp light (beside bed), for lovemaking interlude, which audience can hear. Something is wrong, however, and light is switched back on.* GEORGIA *puts on nightgown,* BURT *puts on pajamas. Both are sitting up in their one bed.)*

GEORGIA: What's the matter?

BURT: I'm worried about Jasper.

GEORGIA: But Burt—why?

BURT: He appears to be crazy.

GEORGIA: On what evidence?

BURT: He wants to end death.

GEORGIA: In that event, we're *all* crazy.

BURT: You mistake me. I mean, Jasper thinks he can pull it off!

GEORGIA: Pull *what* off?

BURT: The trick of eliminating death.

GEORGIA: You mean he's *serious*!?

BURT: Yes, he's as serious as . . .

GEORGIA: Death?

BURT: I'm afraid so. He's also mad at me.

GEORGIA: What did you do to him?

BURT: I was skeptical. I doubted he could do it.

GEORGIA: Do what—end death?

BURT: Precisely.

GEORGIA: *(Enthusiastically, hopefully)* But Burt—what if he's right!?

BURT: Right? About what?

GEORGIA: That he *can* end death! Oh, Burt—what that could mean! Just think! *(Takes* BURT's *hand in hers)* We'd be alive, always!

BURT: *(Skeptically)* How lovely, Georgia. It's just *too* romantic—to be true.

©1982 by Marvin Cohen

GEORGIA: *(Hurt)* Burt! Don't you love me?!

BURT: Of course!

GEORGIA: Forever?

BURT: Naturally.

GEORGIA: *Not* so naturally. Jasper must succeed, first.

BURT: You have a point there. Rather, *two* points. Or rather, *three*.

GEORGIA: Three? *What* three?

BURT: There's *you*.

GEORGIA: *(Counting on her fingers.)* That's one.

BURT: There's *me*.

GEORGIA: *(Counting on her fingers.)* That's two.

BURT: There's our *love*: undying.

GEORGIA: *(Awed)* Love undying! Do you think he can do it?

BURT: Do what? End death?

GEORGIA: Yes, of life and love!

BURT: Not a chance!

GEORGIA: *(Disappointed)* You mean he can't?

BURT: Be realistic.

GEORGIA: *(Weeping)* Goodbye, love.

BURT: *(Clutching her closely)* But not yet!

GEORGIA: *(Weeping)* But *one* day. *(Sobs violently.)*

BURT: Calm yourself. It's Jasper's fault.

GEORGIA: For what?

BURT: For falsely getting your hopes up. You accepted—or were resigned to—our death before. Now, you're all upset.

GEORGIA: I'm sorry. *(She composes herself.)* He's crazy, then?

BURT: Not only that, but vindictively so. Listen to this: He's expelled us from inclusion in his immortality-for-all feast: You and I to be the sole exceptions to an otherwise democratically unexclusive eternal-life gift for every human universally alive enough to be a perpetually grateful recipient of Jasper's landmark endowment: a vital revolution to liven up man's long evolution.

GEORGIA: But Burt—in such largesse, why are *we alone* to be dreadfully cursed as exceptions?

BURT: To punish me, for it was my sin to doubt.

GEORGIA: Doubt that he could ... ?

BURT: Yes, end ...

GEORGIA: ... finally for ever ...

BURT: ... Death.

GEORGIA: But that's cruel—he's your friend!

BURT: No longer. I'm guilty of a high crime: actively sabotaging his proposed abolishment of Death, by virtue of treacherous skepticism, in not lending my moral support. *(Ironically)* But if his invention works out in spite of my "sabotage," then his revenge shall take effect: to deprive you, me, our love—all three—of the everlasting bounty of that impossible invention's humane worldwide munificence in miraculous salvation of all souls physically entire, save ours.

GEORGIA: So we'd be out in the cold?

BURT: Such is Jasper's threat—or, rather, pronouncement. *(Apprehensively looks at her.)* Georgia—*please* don't credit it!

GEORGIA: *(With a glazed look of determined faith)* Jasper passes your understanding. You did wrong, withholding your support. At such great cost!

BURT: At *no* cost, since he won't do what's so strictly impossible.

GEORGIA: *(Poignant, tragic)* But what if it's not!? Our love leaps high with life's blessing. To lose those irreplaceable prizes of love and lives— *(Accusingly)* merely because you doubt! *(Desperately pleading)* Burt, Burt, retract that doubt! Go back to Jasper, and beg his forgiveness! For all our eternal sakes!

BURT: Georgia—you're no more sane or rational than poor Jasper! Surely you can't believe—

GEORGIA: *(Fervently)* But he *might* do it! Impossible or not, he *could* do it!

BURT: *(Defiantly)* Are you on *his* side—or *mine*?

GEORGIA: How can I tell? Yours is reason's side—cold, stoical resignation, with Death waiting surely at the end. *His (Glowingly, fervently, in a leap of piety)* is magic's side, that defies reason by leaping past scientific barriers of realism: the reward for such belief is *(Ecstatically)* Eternity! *(Suddenly switching to worldly suavity.)* That appeal surely is not without a certain undeniable charm?

BURT: Hedging, you want your cake and yet must eat it. How does this dilemma resolve itself?

GEORGIA: Bring before me the discussion you had with Jasper. Set back alive that scene, re-enact its dialogue, as I sit in judgment, choosing between an eternal soul— *(Wistfully ecstatic)* if possible!—or *(Sternly, bravely)* the damnation of cold reason's consoling resignation.

BURT: *(As lights fade)* Well, it was like this. Earlier this very evening itself, I ate out with Jasper. So agitated was he, that—most untypically— he even left some food on his plate. I forget what denomination of food it was, but that's irrelevant to my impression that poor Jasper did seem off his feed. This impression was confirmed when, later, walking along matching strides with me to our club for an after-dinner drink, he would occasionally pause to question the night's air with some pathetic upward glance, looking, for all the world, like a man distracted by the inner disorder of trouble. On arrival at our club, he took familiar bearings there, then proceeded to unravel, bit by bit, what his agitation state strangely owed itself to.

(During this last speech, BURT changes into the clothes he wore to dinner with JASPER. Then he walks to the set of JASPER's living room, even as GEORGIA watches from their bed. She remains as witness to BURT's enactment of flashback, the transition to which may be accompanied by effects and/or music.)

Scene Two

(This scene is told through BURT's point of view; hence, he makes himself appear to be brilliant, realistic, rational: a logician/scientist of humanity and vision. He portrays JASPER as a fanatic, a religious nut completely out of touch with reality.)

(Some time shortly before Scene One. JASPER and BURT, sitting (at conversational distance from each other) in living room of former's apartment. JASPER looks innocent, unworldly. Burt seems more self-possessed and prepared with "all the answers"; low-keyed, often cynical, tastefully negative.)

JASPER: The world is in dreadful shape. What's it coming to?

BURT: Who knows? But once it gets to where it's coming to, it won't stop *there*—it'll plunge right on: right into another generation. You and I, meanwhile, by that time, will be dead.

JASPER: That's what I really hate about life—*mortality*!

BURT: Your hating it is a good sign—shows your values are in the right place.

JASPER: I'm serious, Burt. Now, listen. *(Pause. Recites following two paragraphs with deliberateness and elocution.)*

Something must really be done about death. It's been going much too far, with outrageous consumptive audacity, these very many years! The lives it's claimed! Snatched by so many snares, gobbled up by all matter, manner, and ruse of catastrophe by nature, internal disease, or man-devised means.

Before it's too late, it'll take us all! This scandal is escalating, by outlandish degrees. If we don't soon arrest it—oh!

BURT: *(Reciting dramatically)*
    Eventually, you will die.
    Not to pop into the sky,
    but down in the ground to lie,
    with not the slightest hint of "why."

JASPER: Mock me if you like, Burt. But Death darkly undergoes its concealment: stealthy, patient. Though instantaneously everywhere, Death lurks hidden within and resists all subtle onslaughts to free human life of . . . its secret undoer.

BURT: Secret?! Death is out in the open. By now, it's hardly a secret. Otherwise, why all those long faces you see in the streets and on the buses? They've all caught on, about this death business.

JASPER: Yes, people are dearly fond of life; in time they've learned to hold life as their dearest prize. Nothing's so valuable as each new moment, so fleeting—

BURT: *(Interrupting)* Oh, not so fleeting. Sometimes life lags and flags so slow, as dull monotony endures to tedious boredom. Even *with* our mortal awareness.

(BURT yawns, illustrating his last point; and he might stretch, get up, move about, do something or other, before sitting down again.)

JASPER: But Burt—there's something I must tell you.

BURT: *(Urbanely)* What on Earth can it be? Please, spare me any further suspense. Life is tricky enough, without the upset of unnecessary palpitations. What's on your sleeve—or up your mind? Spill it!

JASPER: Attend: bend your ear: I do intend to outdo Death, at his own game, cut him off, and purge life of its own worst enemy.

Such precisely is the mission I was brought into the world for: my calling I've only just discovered: my ordained task *(Enunciating with deliberateness to emphasize inner rhyme repetition of four "term" sounds.)*, by divine determination: I'm granted a term to terminate our termination.

BURT: Old friend, forgive me: I completely fail to understand.

JASPER: Take me seriously, now. Come under my spell.

BURT: I'd have to be under your spell, to take you seriously.

JASPER: Then let me spell it out for you! It's only too simple. The worst thing about life is that it must end. Why "must" it end? I declare an end to that ending. Death has been in business so long, it must by now have outlived its original purpose—whatever that might have been.

BURT: *(Making JASPER's last phrase into a query and answering it.)* Death's purpose? Shall I tell you? To unclutter the stage and unblock the sun, and clean the halls, and clear the decks, for the free access of newborn generations that come to inherit the works that get passed on to them by those who conveniently leave the stage tidy for the next lot to use.

Be reasonable, dear Jasper. Were death to be abolished (as though it could!), life then would immediately cease to be that dear, lovely, transient, precious, movingly cherished spark of invaluable commodity, unbearably tragic, prized infinitely for its very draining away, beat by beat, as slowly we witness our increasing failure to be a match for a world that gradually fails us, the world we slowly lose as it loses us. Were you to deprive life of its own gradual loss (as though you could!), life would become a contemptuously cheap, banal, wretched, common, tawdry enterprise, open to anyone's ambitious hustle and shoddy self-seeking. Lacking its highest asset—mortality—life would lose value and self-respect; would desire to discard itself: the irony being, that without death, life would find its own shedding difficult to the damning edge of impossibility.

JASPER: Is it possible—what I've heard? Is this the support of a long friendship? Of the whole unwillingly mortal world, are you alone—my old friend—to openly oppose my inspired defiance of death?

BURT: Not I alone. What about our poor undertakers and gravediggers? They have families to support, mouths to feed. Are they to praise you while you deprive them of livelihoods and increase the dismally staggering figures of mass unemployment, thus swelling our swollen economy by increasing the involuntary recruits in the vast, useless army of the out-of-work?

JASPER: *(Impatiently)* Oh, fooey! Cut out the sophistry of your skeptical rhetoric and sour, negative arguments. I appeal to your practical nature, in down-to-earth terms. The main thing is first to do the deed—end death.

BURT: Just like that? How simple! End death? Oh, my! This subject, since time immemorial, has already been thoroughly covered, picked through, and worn out by discussion, fretful worry, and intermittent anxiety. Yet no clueful hint, to date, has been yielded even to patient genius, to saintly brilliance. Then *you* come along, with tonight's agitation that hindered your dinner appetite. You spout a brain-rave: "Do the deed—end death." Historically, the loftiest aim. But *how*, dear boy? Just how?

JASPER: *(Pompously)* Mundane matters of method are but irrelevant vulgarities, when set beside the sublime glory of my pure goal itself. The blazing zeal of faith shall, in its own sweet time, reveal the pedestrian practical matter of mere means. Nor shall I demean, by meanly telling of means, the dear divinity of my faith.

BURT: Let me skeptically persist in asking: What's your method? Alchemistry? Black witchcraft? Mumbo jumbo? Astrological revelation? Revealed truth, by divine visitation?

I know you, Jasper. You're smart in some things, but dumb in science. To dust Death off the human map without resorting to magic of a supernatural kind, you'd have to be up on biology, anatomy, physics, chemistry, organic molecular structure, medicine, right up to the borderline of mystery itself.

JASPER: *(Admitting)* I *am* scientifically ignorant, that's true.

BURT: True? Not merely true! It's a handicap, considering what you propose to do.

JASPER: Handicaps *can* be overcome. They're not all insurmountable.

BURT: *(With heated emphasis)* But in *this* case, your optimism would be the very height of certifiable folly! You've hatched an unworkable scheme. It's unutterably implausible.

JASPER: How do *you* know? Are you an expert?

BURT: *I*'m not. But others are, or were. There've been plenty. Genius has been in no short supply: Population and time, on our rotund global sphere charged with history, have abundantly seen to that. Great minds have abounded. They've tackled many problems, plowed into the thickets of mystery on pioneering tractors that cultivated wilderness into hygienic sophistication and refined our primitive fear. Longevity has inched ahead; yet Death itself, with its borders mildly retracted, slightly retrenched, remains ever grimly, monstrously, mythically, in an ironbound control over the fragile, swaying destiny of each proud mortal.

JASPER: But Burt—that was before *I* was reckoned on.

BURT: Are you, then, of Christlike proportion, to historically create a new tide on our astronomical surface?

JASPER: I'm a major figure. My advent is nigh. I've arrived.

BURT: And with you—the era of the immortals?

JASPER: *(Darkly)* We'll see.

BURT: As you're not getting any younger, you'd better get to work.

JASPER: Don't harass me. I only conceived my plan this evening. Why the rush? What's to be, comes on apace. It's in the works. We're swooped down on. And you can help.

BURT: *(Incredulous)* Now really! *I*?! How?

JASPER: By having faith.

BURT: Jasper, you're being exceedingly silly.

JASPER: Don't bully me. Have faith.

BURT: Death is not a person to be conquered. It's a built-in condition—

JASPER: *(Cutting in; violently)* Shut up! Have faith!

BURT: Tempered by pity and loyalty, I patiently refrain from exploding at the driven pathos of your drivel. I contend that faith—in which you put your hope—does *not*, contrary to that hope, conquer all.

JASPER: *Prove* that blasphemy, you sacrilegious cur!

BURT: *(Lightheartedly, despite* JASPER's *outbursts of violent insult.)* A world-famous example is Joan of Arc, whose burning zeal led to her own burning squeal. Her saint-like faith didn't keep her goose from being cooked and done to a turn, giving her a fatal burn, when more than her faith was at stake. Her heroic faith led to her making an ash of herself. From a *member* of the devout, she became an *ember.* We'll go to Islam for our next example. The more Mohammed prayed, the more the mountain remained just where it was, in stony stubbornness.

The Crusades—all that human effort fueled by holy hope—ended the day of many a dazed knight with the bleak blight of an endless night.

JASPER: Are you troubling yourself to inform me that faith cannot conquer all? Don't bother dredging more examples from the teeming archives of the past. You may cite failure after failure from legend and history, the sorry lot that befell the stubborn strife of high endeavor. Argue endlessly that faith cannot conquer all. The point is: Mine *will!* *(He's been reaching a stage of turbulent frenzy and fanatical mayhem.)*

BURT: You're a holy fake.

JASPER: *(Piously)* I forgive you. You know not what you say. But you're too ignorant not to say it.

BURT: *(Still lighthearted, but generous-mindedly concerned, worried, solicitous.)* You're not even in your own control, but you're a man possessed of "a faith worse than death." Or perhaps you're stubbornly sticking to your guns in order to "save faith." You exceed your own sane boundary, and rove wildly outside the old Jasper I've known as a friend: the mock pretender of the "you" known and loved by me for years.

JASPER: *(In mounting wrath)* For your flippant attempt to misguide me, using the name of friendship unfriendily, using trust untrustworthily, to slip me evil advice to renege on my divine inspired calling—I call you my enemy, my worm in friend's guise; and I call on you to backtrack and apologize with humiliating humility.

BURT: If I don't?

JASPER: Then, I'll exclude you and your Georgia from the Eternity feast to which everyone else is warmly only too welcome. You and your love shall be the sole poor exemptions from my Universal Liberation and Salvation Program. You'll go uninvited! *(In vindictive wrath)* How I relish this pronouncement!

BURT: Jasper, please! Don't give way—

JASPER: *(Interrupting)* You dare prevent me from achieving my mission by withholding your moral support? That's sabotage—traitor! With the authority entrusted in me—from sources I prefer at this time not to divulge—I pronounce, on you and Georgia—Death!

BURT: You'd murder us?

JASPER: No: you'd live out your "normal" lifetimes—without entitlement to my New Dispensation.

BURT: Your insane delusions border on the frenzy and mayhem of a pseudo-semblance of mock violence.

JASPER: *(Amused, undaunted, superior)* What a quaint accusation! Let me remind you, my former friend, that the material deaths of you and Georgia will be automatically fatal to the spiritual *Love* that binds you two together in an enduring blaze of passion.

BURT: Whereas, the love between you and your Ginger will partake of your joint personal immortalities?

JASPER: *(His megalomania showing)* Quite! *Our* love survives, in glorious plenitude, outlasting the obsolete datedness of mere former mechanical time.

You scoff—all *you*'re capable of is to be *against*. Well, *I*'m against our hitherto unbeatable adversary. Death so far has proved inevitable on the field of combat, and has gone undefeated, taking on all comers. There's where *I* come in, as history's special agent, and evolution's hidden spy. I'm Life's secret weapon, in a surprise attack. I'm on my mark, ripe and hot and raring to go—ready for the kill. I'm roused to my task, divinely guided to a firm girding of living loins placed stupendously to the test. *(Spews out)* May my great scheme survive your horrid little opposition, and greatly prevail: your death-loving venom notwithstanding!

BURT: No scheme—ineffectual dream.

JASPER: *(Livid with demonic, furious rage)* Then *die, die, die,* you—

BURT: *(Calmly interrupting)* You have strange ideas. You theorize without foundation, then accuse me of disloyalty in friendship just because I honestly proclaim my misgivings as to just how tenable your life-perpetuation proposition sincerely seems to me. As of now, your craziness has impaired our friendship. I will now leave you, to return to a happier prospect—my dear Georgia. *(Begins to start to leave. Firmly, solemnly, in grim warning.)* Alone, perhaps, you'll reconsider just what's in your power and what's not. The potent "magic" of your wish, however passionately felt, is only an unseen mental thought. Its manifestation *would* be Death's end. But that thought's *actual* manifestation is—simply put—your temporary leaving of your senses; or rather, your senses' leaving of you. Sensibly, I do too. Good-bye.

(BURT comes over to JASPER; he tries to restrain, comfort, or calm JASPER by putting his former familiar friendly arm around JASPER; but JASPER squirms out and abruptly flings the proffered embrace-arm away.)

JASPER: *(Hatefully, spiteful, loathing)* Get away!

BURT: Jasper, I fear that you're mad.

JASPER: I am—at *you!* *(While BURT leaves.)* Die, you faithless former friend turned foe: die, die, die, die: most emphatically die . . . *(In strident raucousness, obsessedly incoherent)*

(BURT has left.)

JASPER: *(Alone now; standing, shifting about, restless, resolute, determined, offended, smarting.)* He'll rue that speech: he'll eat it. May my venture succeed. On it hangs so much. Going to the moon was once a miracle: Now, it's only history.

(Upon exiting, BURT has re-entered his own bedroom, changed back to pajamas, and re-joined GEORGIA in bed in time for Scene Three. Blackout on JASPER.)

Scene Three

(BURT, in pajamas, and GEORGIA, in nightgown, both sitting up in one bed as before, at end of Scene One.)

BURT: There: that's what took place between us. I'm able to include in my thorough report his final soliloquy, having eavesdropped on it after walking out to conclude our dialogue. Scientific curiosity, and concern for a deranged old friend, justify my sneaky snooping: which also helps to round out this report I file, to completely inform you; as I abide, I hope, your verdict kind to me.

(Kisses GEORGIA, who receives it passively, or obliviously.)

GEORGIA: God!—all these years I've known Jasper—who would have expected it of him!?

(GEORGIA means that she never would have guessed JASPER could ever be such a nobly brilliant visionary of courage; BURT mistakes her meaning: he thinks she means she never thought that JASPER would ever lose his mind and go crazy.)

BURT: *(Charitably)* He's not dangerous—to himself or to anyone else. Alone, he grapples in the grip of a grandiose idea—his back turned on the collective commonplace shallow sanity of his fellow men. Let him wrestle with what has taken full possession of his deranged senses. He'll lose, and then—bowed, subdued, humble, modest, he'll return to us his friends and partake of our plain and simple aspirations, the bounty of our doomed and mortal kind.

(Turns off bedside lamp on his side.) Enough about *him*—it's too pathetic to think about. Let's return to each other, where it's healthier. Switch your light off, now. *(Suggestively)* Let me grope for you—and you for me—by amorous touch and feel. *(Makes advance and pass.)*

GEORGIA: *(Keeping the table lamp on her side on; totally ignoring BURT's innuendo and advances.)* Oh Burt—what a sublime, supreme, noble, glorious goal Jasper is consumed by. It's too anguishing—it's wrenchingly poignant—to think that he must fail. *(Pause. In dreamlike quavering.)* But should his salvation-for-everyone scheme succeed in the face of your disbelief, Jasper has condemned us to unique deaths. Infidelity and treachery deserve no less than the death penalty. Why should my innocent life share your awful fate? I terminate, then my alliance with your coldly reasoning, irreverently rational cause; and switch to him, however fanatical or futile his storming the fortress that guards the dark secret of Death's final word over human life.

BURT: Be plain—is it him or me?

GEORGIA: Let your grief flow.

BURT: But Georgia—we're in love—remember?

GEORGIA: Our love is surely doomed if I remain with you. It's finite: We're condemned to death, without mercy, by our lord Jasper. He's my salvation—you're my damnation. I transfer affection convert to the winning side. I'm now Jasper's devotee.

BURT: You're like Jasper—out of control. Let me caution you—as in vain I cautioned him—to level down your passionate peaks from that heady atmosphere where fulfillment frantically follows and tumbles in an agonized reeling to keep up with the spiral of inflated dreams, the balloon voyage from which fulfillment must bail out and plunge—parachuteless—to its absolute wreckage on the plains of hard sense.

GEORGIA: Burt—our love is dead!

BURT: *(Alarmed)* No!—not that!

GEORGIA: *Jasper* shares my soul—you *never* can.

BURT: Georgia, you're abandoning me? Our love was developed over a long time, in organic stress and trial. Now, in a wayward perversion and superstitious dread of Death, you toss aside our sacred love, to share the faith of Jasper's folly, in your protective dash of maternal pity for so vulnerably insane a self-proclaimed Saviour of scientific ineptitude.

GEORGIA: *(During following section, she's gradually changing into street clothes and packing her small bag.)* I follow my heart! Is that clear enough? He's the better man, Burt. By far. He looks far. You accept the mean near. By your own recounting, he came to life—at your expense. Your reason paled to brittleness, while my heart went out to his soul that flowed free from the man-made manacles of petty reason that shackles itself to the miserable confines of reality.

BURT: But Jasper isn't free—he's possessed! He's chained! He's deluded!

GEORGIA: He fights Death. Cravenly, you accept it.

BURT: He's *against* Death, but how can he fight it? It's unopposable.

GEORGIA: *(In finality and loathing)* Burt, you're a physical materialist. I hate to think that a body belonging to such a mind ever made love to mine. I'll purge your body from mine, in the violated shrine of my memory, by alliance with noble Jasper!

BURT: You forget: he already loves and is loved—by Ginger.

GEORGIA: I'll easily relieve her of him.

BURT: *(Anguished)* No! Say you're joking! Put out this sudden nightmare, and let sensible light illumine our resumed sanity!

GEORGIA: Though Ginger's been with Jasper for years in living love, I'll supplant her and take over. Nothing—but nothing!—will stand in the way of my deathless newfound passion: joining missions with humanity's crusading Saviour in his vast, miraculous campaign to conquer that bane of life—the worm of death. *(Carried away)* Death: the fly in humanity's ointment. The rotten apple in mankind's contentedness barrel. The black lining on an otherwise spotless horizon. Our ancient, and still-going-strong, nemesis: Death, the dread of which has given rise to religion, metaphysics, the occult, magic, superstition, astral speculation, tragedy, drama, art, philosophy, music, literature, romance, and idealism. Death: the eternal worm slowly trickling through the core of our pathetic, body-based egoes.

(BURT tries to keep her from packing.)

GEORGIA: Out of my way, scum. You're far behind my life, already.

BURT: So Georgia—we're done?

GEORGIA: Goodbye, you defective man. I leave you to the lonely solace of your reason. Our love is now a warm corpse. In breath and beat of heart, our love has gone still. From this burial, a new love leaps for me: for Jasper, and his noble crusade to wage war in a holy match against Death, a mortal combat with me racing to be his ally or nurse or lieutenant or assistant, ministering to his distress or to his glory, in his unarmed fight to the very finish.

BURT: "Unarmed" is right. He'll prove a pushover for Death. *You'*ll topple, alongside: the foolish warrior, and his silly bride.

GEORGIA: We'll see!

(In a burst of determination, GEORGIA finally bolts past BURT's physical barrier-like resistance, and exits. BURT is left standing there, sharply outlined in the shock of sudden loneliness, unloved.)

BURT: Has the world caved in and gone mad? Logic has bolted, rationality fled, leaving only me to piece together broken remnants and shattered debris. Are things totally out of hand, beyond repair? Maybe normality and order can reclaim themselves, through me alone, as their abandoned agent. Resolutely, I'll follow Georgia, trace her fugitive flight to Jasper's house; there she'll make a scene, joining nonsenses with her model in madness. I'll enter and make my own scene, to undo, forestall, or curb their compounded foolish danger. I must avert their double doom, and repair my desperate loss of Georgia: who, in her *right* mind, is my life's fit companion, my love's double—if only I can patch the leak and unleak the flood from the violent crack of her stability.

(Exits, in desperate resolve, in same direction as GEORGIA'S recent flight.)

Scene Four

(Very dim lights at top, just to distinguish from blackout. Sounds of attempted lovemaking, which stop prematurely because lovemaking is unsuccessful. Pause. Lamp is switched on by JASPER: revealing bedroom of JASPER and GINGER. This bedroom is seen in typical state of disarray, giving very different feeling from BURT's bedroom.)

(Time is shortly earlier than time of preceding scene. JASPER is not as BURT had portrayed him, being far calmer, though still a visionary type. JASPER, having put on pajamas, and GINGER, having put on nightgown, are now sitting up in their bed.)

GINGER: What's the matter?

JASPER: I'm worried about Burt.

GINGER: But Jasper—why?

JASPER: He appears to be crazy.

GINGER: On what evidence?

JASPER: He won't oppose that worst of all evils—Death. In addition to which, moreover, he betrayed me by cutting off the usual loyal support I've always expected from him.

GINGER: But what does that first point have to do with the second? Really, Jasper, I'm still quite in the dark, despite your just having turned on the light.

JASPER: *(Putting his arm around* GINGER.*)* Oh, let's drop the whole complicated, confounded matter. It's beneath our tired consideration, and besides, is rather unsavory.

GINGER: Let's *not* drop this whole matter. I'm getting fascinated, if not yet intrigued. Now, what's this business between you and Burt?

JASPER: He has a phony mask of slick, level-headed confidence, on a plane of superficial materiality. His spiritual void is thinly layered over by a veneer of shallow cynicism.

GINGER: How can you so slight him—an old friend?

JASPER: He just refuses to go along with me on this new scheme I've concocted—an immensely practical, desperately needed scheme.

GINGER: *What* scheme?

JASPER: I intend to free all people from their own very worst enemy, which spoils their happiness and ruins their lives.

GINGER: And what may *that* be?

JASPER: Life's arch-rival: Death itself.

GINGER: You can't be serious?

JASPER: I *am*—as serious as . . .

GINGER: Death?

JASPER: You named that dread word!

GINGER: Be sensible—how on Earth, *how?*

JASPER: Ginger—that's exactly what I objected to in Burt; and you're sounding just like him.

GINGER: It's a reasonable question—from him *or* from me.

JASPER: Please, Ginger—one Burt is enough. In fact, *too* much. Don't *you* go imitating what I already find too intolerable in *him.* Losing him is bad enough. Losing you—I couldn't recover from it. So take care. *(He turns out his bedside lamp light.)* Just go on loving me, and extend your love to my new idea as well, without the interference of a questioning and doubting attitude. *(Turns off light and kisses* GINGER *passionately.)*

GINGER: *(Breaking the embrace.)* Curiosity now intrigues me confoundingly. I'd like to hear the whole story. How did your bitter dispute start, which ended in such upset, with dear old allies so at odds apart?

JASPER: Since you insist, I'll now illuminate you. *(Turns on his lamp light.)* But recounting what happened seems pointlessly not worth the trouble, in view of Burt's dastardly, knavish, cutthroat defiance of an idea too beautifully humane even to contest.

GINGER: *Please* indulge me—it's a whim, but I must hear all.

JASPER: Then prepare yourself, dear Ginger. You'll end up agreeing how hateful Burt is, and how lovable I. And you'll embrace my marvelous scheme.

GINGER: Divulge! Hold back no longer.

JASPER: *(As lights fade)* Well, it was like this. Earlier this very evening itself, I ate out with Burt. So inspired was I, that—most untypically— I even left some food on my plate. I forget what denomination of food it was, but that's irrelevant to my sublime conviction that I really had something great up here *(Points to his own head.)* to chew on. This conviction was confirmed when, later, walking along matching strides with Burt to our club for an after-dinner drink, I would occasionally pause to question the night's air with some ecstatic upward glance, detecting ample signs favorably prophetic to my divinely ordained mission. On arrival at our club, I took familiar bearings there, then proceeded to unravel, but by bit, what my inspiration state so elatedly owed itself to.

(During this last speech, JASPER changes into the clothes he wore to dinner with BURT. Then he walks to the living room set, even as GINGER watches from their bed. She remains as witness to JASPER's re-enactment of flashback, the transition to which may be accompanied by effects and/or music.)

Scene Five

(BURT and JASPER at latter's apartment, sitting at conventional distance from each other in living room. Identical setting to that of Scene Two. This scene, however, is told through JASPER's eyes. Hence JASPER appears to be a far-sighted visionary: the ultimate, passionate visionary; a benevolent philanthropist willing to dedicate all his energy in a self-sacrificing effort to free mankind from bondage to death. BURT, on the other hand, is made to appear petty, cynical, bitchy, negative.)

JASPER: The world is in dreadful shape. What's it coming to?

BURT: Who knows? But once it gets to where it's coming to, it won't stop *there*—it'll plunge right on: right into another generation. You and I, meanwhile, by that time, will be dead.

JASPER: That's what I really hate about life—*mortality!*

BURT: Your hating it is a good sign—shows your values are in the right place.

JASPER: I'm serious, Burt. Now, listen. *(Pause. Recites following two paragraphs with deliberateness and elocution.)*
　　Something must really be done about death. It's been going much too far, with outrageous consumptive audacity, these very many years! The lives it's claimed! Snatched by so many snares, gobbled up by all matter, manner, and ruse of catastrophe by nature, internal disease, or mandevised means.
　　Before it's too late, it'll take us all! This scandal is escalating, by outlandish degrees. If we don't soon arrest it—oh!

BURT: *(Reciting in a sing-song)*
　　Eventually, you will die.
　　Not to pop into the sky,
　　but down in the ground to lie,
　　with not the slightest hint of "why."

JASPER: Mock me if you like, Burt. But Death darkly undergoes its concealment: stealthy, patient. Though instantaneously everywhere, Death lurks hidden within and resists all subtle onslaughts to free human life of . . . its secret undoer.

BURT: Secret?! Death is out in the open. By now, it's hardly a secret. Otherwise, why all those long faces you see in the streets and on the buses? They've all caught on, about this death business.

JASPER: Yes, people are dearly fond of life; in time they've learned to hold life as their dearest prize. Nothing's so valuable as each new moment, so fleeting—

BURT: *(Interrupting)* Oh, not so fleeting. Sometimes life lags and flags so slow, as dull monotony endures to tedious boredom. Even *with* our mortal awareness.

*(*BURT *yawns, illustrating his last point; and he might stretch, get up, move about, do something or other, before sitting down again.)*

JASPER: But Burt—there's something I must tell you.

BURT: *(Sarcastically)* What on Earth can it be? Please, spare me any further suspense. Life is tricky enough, without the upset of unnecessary palpitations. What's on your sleeve—or up your mind? Spill it!

JASPER: Attend: bend your ear: I do intend to outdo Death, at his own game, cut him off, and purge life of its own worst enemy.
　　Such precisely is the mission I was brought into the world for: my calling I've only just discovered: my ordained task *(Enunciating with deliberateness to emphasize inner rhyme repetition of four "term" sounds.)*

by divine determination: I'm granted a term to terminate our termination.

BURT: If this is a joke, what's the punch line?

JASPER: I've never been this serious before.

BURT: Then, justify yourself. It's late, I want to go home. Georgia's waiting.

JASPER: So has everyone so far been: for their mortal end. But I'm putting an end to that wait. *(Pause)* I don't intend idly to stand by like all our other doomed sheep, to watch Death gradually unfold its malice with decomposing cells, physical decay, bodily rot, working insidiously from within like a Trojan Horse of classical treachery or deception.

BURT: *(With arch cynicism)* So *you* are to be history's very first circum venter, forestaller, arrester, outwitter, and ultimate undoer of our pro lific devastator, Death?

JASPER: I confess to that purpose.

BURT: With what means, at hand?

JASPER: My goal will find its instrument, my aim its tool, my crusade its revelation.

BURT: That sounds evasive.

JASPER: I evade nothing. Open-eyed, I take deliberate aim. Like an an tiquated monster of pestilence that should have been shuffled off in pre historic obsolescence, Death has been around too long for our own good as a species. It should long ago have been dispatched, in a merciless act of enlightened mercy. By my ready hands I'll do now what the rusty hands of the human race have been overdue to do. To outdo Death— our deliverance so dormant, so latent. Better dormant, than a doormat Better latent than never. By my ready hand and deadly eye—

BURT: *(Cutting in)* Your stalking Death as a prey is an act of foolish idiocy. Low on sense, you resort to a senseless profusion of *words*, that reproduce like rabbits drugged with aphrodisiacs and deprived of birth control methods—just like *you're* deprived of *death*-control methods you hare-brain! You're comic, not cosmic.

JASPER: *(Visionarily)* I behold it: a secular Last Judgment, with blessings of paradisical enormity on literally a global scale. Life in its own ab solute magnitude: Life of incontestable virtue in itself. To compound Life by infinity, to unstop it of mortal limits, to eternalize its stupendous essence in a riot of abundance to the superlative excess of an extremely good thing, would be to place our happiness, our dignity, on a scale of imperishability, in a daily delight of an endless treasure. The world shall be a stage for lovers—sweet lovers, in spring's tide; and lovers will dally forever.

BURT: *(Bluntly, annihilatingly practical; thus negatingly)* Frankly, I doubt it. It's late, Georgia is waiting.

JASPER: *(Still glowing, full-blast, in spite of* BURT'*s negative tone.)* Everyone, you and your Georgia included, is warmly ever so welcome to my lavishly programmed Eternity Feast. The loves you and your Georgia feel for each other, the loves that link Ginger and me, all true bonds, shall now, with the magnitude of a new bounty, partake of our joint personal immortalities. Should my scheme's grand potential succeed as planned, its humane strategy is devised to prolong indefinitely each marvelous illustration of the human condition.

Numbly, our society in all its customs has succumbed to tragedy—chronicling it but barely opposing it. Death is the invisible breeder of tragedy, working with all its cunning maggots to secretly separate our cells from the wholesome healthy radiance that sings the vibrant song of life. Let life now celebrate its liberation from what undermines its fiery self! Let the world throb with its genius, Life! Let life finally command its continuity! Let it build a pedestal to the purity and praise of an indwelling permanence!

BURT: *(Sarcastically)* How lovely it sounds, my dear Jasper! How I'd dearly love to be in your debt—to join all other no-longer-mortals in a rejoicing, jubilant cry of endless gratitude. Alas, I fear that being obligated to you will not be my great fortune—nor my Georgia's, nor your Ginger's, nor anyone's—due to your not coming through on your vaunted promise.

JASPER: I give you my supreme Word! To the old Creation I'll affix an amendment—a royal addition, a crucial editorial revision!

Whatever extraordinary or divine means this entails, I'll make it my uncanny business—if I haven't already done so—to find; and somehow put to work, so as to take effect: *(Apocalyptically)* Then— *(Pause for suspense)* soon Behold! *(Raises his arms and circles slowly)* Oh, how can you decline into a wet-blanket whining killjoy, in the face of the immense challenge I've undertaken? My friend—

(JASPER tries to put his arm around BURT in a gesture of friendliness and an attempt to include BURT in JASPER's messianic glow and ardent fervor—but BURT angrily thrusts the proffered arm—and JASPER—away, with violent, scornful rejection.)

JASPER: Burt—you thrust me aside? As my best friend, in my hour of crucial need, you should be dishing out love and support unstintingly.

BURT: As your best friend, I'm only telling you some dreary truths. Your phoniness is betrayed verbally. Your choice of words is abominable. Your rhetoric abounds with shameless patches of purple. Not only don't people think like you—they don't even talk like you. You're out of touch—you're remote from the fabric and fiber of others, their pulse and gristle, their beat and thump. So as a friend, I should be supporting you? In defying what's sacred to you, I deny all of you? In your time of need, do I prove a false friend? Can I be so petty or spiteful, to despise your ultimate mission to rescue humanity and redeem our universe?

How too true! It's my confessed crime. Gaily, I exempt my conscience from the stain of any guilt. I don't even deign to care!

JASPER: *(In calm holiness)* Notwithstanding those words, I confer on you, your Georgia, and every living other person, a lifetime of permanence in the beautiful universe of existence. There, love and life both grow ever endless.

BURT: Cut out that dopey bribery. Georgia and I will die. So will, therefore, that third entity: the love that binds Georgia and me. The three of us—Georgia, I, and the love between us—are bound, despite you and your drippy benevolence, to die—die—die!

JASPER: Mock me all you wish—on *your* account. But, gallantly, for your dear Georgia's sake, shouldn't you shelter her, protect her, from joining your doom down the gloomy river of a death-wish?

BURT: Even to the River Styx she sticks with me—quite nonexempt, in reasonable resignation to the most inevitable force of existence: life's sure demise.

JASPER: Joined in love, she shares equally the folly of your blunder?

BURT: Yes. Heartless, aren't I? I've signed her death-warrant. A suicidal pact between lovers!

JASPER: *(In noble compassion)* Poor Georgia! I'd never treat her that way if she were *mine*! Ginger's luckier, by far!

BURT: I really must go. Georgia's been expecting me. My death-acceptance speech must, like life itself and love itself, end. Dying, I'll go join my dying love—while we're still young enough to be sexy and vital.

JASPER: Dear would-be betrayer! How you'll come to realize your error, once you live to see that what you call my "dream" has come to be performed on the real, real stage! Only the true drama shall convince you. How ripe the theatre readies, to rehearse its never-ending climax! O bold scheme! Turn my perfect faith to joy and triumph. Turn spectators into actors, to perform everlastingly. Let life realize deathlessness, to perfection! Then doubt is ousted, along with its dire source, Death. For then, all blessings shall excel. Farewell!

(He exits.)

BURT: To contradict your bloated dream's futility, in blunt finality:

Georgia and I will die, and so will you. And love will die as we do. Let me repeat. "Die, die, die!"

Not only will we and love all die, but before all that, our friendship precedes those deaths, and is the first to die. Let our friendship's death be your rehearsal for *stronger* stuff! It will harden you, yet!

(As he's concluding this speech, JASPER is changing back into his pajamas and rejoining GINGER in their bed for Scene Six.)

Scene Six

(Same setting as for Scene Four: JASPER, in pajamas, and GINGER, in nightgown, both sitting up in same bed.)

JASPER: That, alas, is what took place, my darling Ginger.

GINGER: I'm so glad you told me. Now I know.

JASPER: Know what, my dear?

GINGER: *(Springing her surprise)* That you and I, you jerk, are through!

JASPER: *(Incredulous)* What have I heard?!

GINGER: In your strongly biased version that purported to report your rather polarized conversation with Burt, I could see through your glaring effort at self-glorification. You maligned a sensibly respectable man, unjustly portraying him as a nit-picking, negative ingrate. You contemptibly failed to render him contemptible. Your scheme to strip our mortal world of mortality is precisely what Burt criticized it to be: the sheerest hokum, an out-and-out work of nonsensical fraudulence. I'm ashamed to have been associated with you in so-called love.

JASPER: Our love was patiently built up over years . . .

GINGER: Now an issue has come on which to sever our bond by driving home a basic incompatibility. Let us now agree on only one thing: to part. To that extent, our love harmoniously ends.

JASPER: *(Desperately)* But my darling!—

GINGER: *(As though waking up)* I'm a realist. It's unreasonable to try to end death. What was I doing, loving *(Contemptuously) you* all this time? It was crazy of me. By getting rid of you, I'm happily rational now. Next man, I'll know better.

JASPER: *(Urgently)* I beg you!

GINGER: *(As though to herself)* Burt and I are realists: passively resigned, fortified by stoical reasoning, to death's ultimate, conclusively unconquerable eventuality. That paragon of worldly reasonableness, the coolly level-headed, calmly down-to-earth Burt, is now the only possible man for me. After years of you, he's the surest antidote. I hold you in a total abhorrence. Make way. *(During this speech, she'd been getting out of bed and dressing.)*

JASPER: *(Alarmed, miserably upset)* Don't desert me! I need you!

GINGER: However, *I* need *you* not.

JASPER: That was the accurate Burt I took the pains to depict. His shallow narrowness of spirit—if you throw yourself away on *him*—you'd be shrunk to his size!

(Unheeding JASPER's passionately desperate protest, GINGER has meanwhile been dressing decisively.)

JASPER: *(Hysterical)* Reconsider! At stake—

(GEORGIA suddenly bursts into the room, interrupting JASPER in mid-apoplectic outburst. She shows a different kind of agitation than JASPER's, being passionately positively in the thrall of his (now hers as well) death-conquering vision mania.)

GEORGIA: *(Puffing, gloriously out of breath)* I see, Ginger, that you've been dressing to go out. Don't go just yet. I have a most vital announcement to make—of direct bearing on the core of our changing lives.

GINGER: *(With deliberate calmness and chilling composure, putting the finishing touches on her going-out dressing-grooming.)* "On the core of our changing lives." Dear me. Whatever can it be? *(Ironically)* Please spare me further suspense. I wait with all the breathlessness of death.

GEORGIA: *(Looking at, motioning ardently to, JASPER.)* Ginger, that man I'm pointing to is kindred to my very soul. Nothing—least of all you— shall stand in our holy union's way. I'm now divine Jasper's devoted apprentice, in deathless support of his undying devastation of that old devastater, dire Death.

GINGER: In other words, you're a fool. It's a case of a fool being attracted to another. As though two fools together would undo each one's foolishness. Ah, if mathematics were only that simple!

GEORGIA: You insult us both!

GINGER: You're already so possessive and joined with him. As though *two* quests to kill death would turn the trick, in the stead of merely one.

Let me personally invite you to get the hell out of here. One of you is bad enough: Two quite tops my very limit.

GEORGIA: What you mean with that rude invective, which you put so indirectly, is simply that you refuse to give up Jasper to me—isn't that it? But by ordinance of God (or His equivalent in these unpious times), Jasper's now mine. If to win him I'll have to fight, then fight I will. So purely purposed is my desperate might to take what's mine, I'll resort to force—like this— *(GEORGIA has swung her large, heavy bag, in violence, at GINGER's head.)*

GINGER: *(Ducking) (Gloating)* Missed! You cracked idealist! You lousy hunk of death-fright!

(GEORGIA swings her bag, with violence, a second time at GINGER.)

GINGER: *(Again ducking)* Again missed, you whore to insanity! You camp-following groupie to the magnetic irrational!

(Seething, with murderous intent, GEORGIA swings her bag for the third time, in vicious violence—harder than ever. Just at that moment, BURT has entered.)

GINGER: *(Distracted by her affectionate discovery on seeing her new love, BURT, thus forgetting to duck.)* Burt! Burt!

BURT: *(In complete surprise)* Why, Ginger!

(Just as BURT replies "Why, GINGER!", the violently swung-directed bag lands with a hard thud on GINGER's head. Collapsing, she remains motionless on floor where fallen. BURT and JASPER are stunned. BURT frantically attempts to revive GINGER, but fails. Hurriedly, GEORGIA extracts a mirror from her purse and holds it under GINGER's nose.)

BURT: *(Anxiously, to GEORGIA)* Well?

GEORGIA: *(In tense disappointment)* Not the slightest fog of cloud on this mirror!

BURT: *(Alarmed)* Then her nose isn't giving any breath?

JASPER: *(Anguished at encountering premature mundane banal situational example of his lofty abstract chosen opponent.)* Is she—O dreadful, un-thinkable—"dead"?!

GEORGIA: *(In horror)* Damn it, it looks like it! No breathing is indicated on this slick, slick, smooth mirror surface!

(GEORGIA and the two men now start to panic.)

BURT: What can we do!?

JASPER: Just what *I* was wondering.

GEORGIA: Here's your brilliant chance, my divine new-found Jasper, to give an advance sample of your greater later full-scale campaign.

JASPER: But how, my sudden Georgia?

GEORGIA: Vindicate by an early example the courageous soundness of your daring mission against *all* of death, by making a raid in particular against the precisely specific possible danger that *Ginger* is here now, thanks to me, dead.

JASPER: But Georgia—I may not be ready! My plan was projected—

GEORGIA: *(Urgently interrupting)* Come down prematurely to Earth, from your vast onslaught of your projections. Here lies Ginger. Apply the earliest advance of your grand and wholesale remedy, in her concrete case, at once!

JASPER: *(Sputtering with alarm)* Too soon! My calculations—

GEORGIA: *(Interrupting; supplicates, genuflects, worshipfully embraces her new idol.)* Save universal humanity; but before you do, make a swift trial practice run, against the hastily roused mortality of poor endangered Ginger, there in her morbid state. I vow my love in support. Show a hint of what's to come. *(Seeing JASPER display obvious fright-stagger.)* Pluck at the talent source of your magic gift, humbly now to perform!

JASPER: *(Pathetically inadequate to GEORGIA's strong plea.)(Whining, petulant)* Whatever miracle you expect, I'm not up to, at present.

BURT: *(To GEORGIA)* You see, Georgia: I told you, but you wouldn't believe me; he's showing his flying colors as a craven phony. It was all wind—he can't do a thing! Phoning for an emergency hospital ambulance would be infinitely wiser than to place, in the hysterical impotence of our panic, reliance on a charlatan's homeopathic self-proclaimed spiritualist hocum.

GEORGIA: *(Dismissingly)* Much too late, by now, to resort to so prosaic an expediency as to phone for emergency hospital ambulance service. Either Jasper comes through by divine miracle's merciful agency, or the ghost is up.

BURT: Let's face it plainly: the poor girl is dead. Being Jasper's girlfriend (or technically *former* girlfriend if she's dead, not to raise too fine a point on it), then she's *Jasper's* responsibility (although with the airs he puts on, do you call that responsibility?). Anyway, incompetent though he may be, it's *his* affair—not ours. But you and I, Georgia, quick!, let's leave this sticky mess before we get too involved! Let's get out of here!

GEORGIA: But we already *are* involved! Or, rather, it's *me* who's involved; after all, damn it, aren't I the one who killed her? For that, I must face, however onerous or unpleasant, the key responsibility for the abominable atrocity of poor lifeless Ginger's lying there *(Gesturing toward GINGER)*, pathetically translated to a precocious corpsehood from the customary lively quickness that characterizes normal city life.

BURT: Let's run away, Georgia! There's the devil to pay!

GEORGIA: *(Derisively)* Theology from *you*, Burt? I'm surprised! As the one who killed her, poor dear, she's *my* responsibility: which, imploringly, I pass on now to a man built in a hero mold—Jasper: Perform heroism, O brave one!

JASPER: *(Hangdog)* As I said before—I'm just not up to that line of work tonight; I'm off my game; the mood just isn't on me.

GEORGIA: Not inspired? Waiting to work up enthusiasm? Brooding on your Muse?

JASPER: Must I confess to fear?

The chips are down, but I choke up in the clutch. When it comes down to the crunch, I'm asked to perform a simple resurrection by retroactive resuscitation. That's all I need do. And yet— *(In pathetic futile impotence; confessing)* I simply can't!

GEORGIA: *(With reluctance, mocking)* "I simply can't!" You say that looking woefully constipated. If this weren't a life-or-death matter, there would be comical overtones—

JASPER: *(Admitting)* All abject, my true colors cowardly come crawling through. *(Covers his face with his hands in classical posture of shame, theatrically overdone.)* Oh, my ignominy!

GEORGIA: *(Furious, impassioned)* In the person—lying there—of poor Ginger, your girlfriend till now: Death—your chosen nemesis—turns, for once, real. Your abstractly humanitarian antideath posture, so bravely declared and proclaimed by yourself that I too have fallen for it, is now exposed and debunked in clear view.

My love, so new, dissolves in a shame of tears and disgust, beholding craven weakness where strength promised brazen in your bold show of old words. Oh, phew!

JASPER: *(Who, except for his brief attempt with GEORGIA and BURT to revive GINGER, has remained sitting up in bed all this time since scene's beginning. Now reduced to a terrified hiding under the sheets. In muffled but nevertheless clearly audible voice.)* No, I just can't! Oh, the horror of death!

BURT: Jasper, try, I beg you! Just try, at least!

JASPER: What?!

GEORGIA: You?!

(JASPER and GEORGIA staring in surprise at this unexpected source.)

BURT: I now retract everything I said, in belittling your powers of miracle. I was being glibly negative by prejudice: for such flippancy, please forgive. Now Ginger is in a state of moribund emergency; do *attempt* her resurrection, Jasper: give it your all. Should you restore her languid cadaver to the shining health of life and fortune, I shall then declare my personally permanent allegiance, and join your League and Legion of lively stalwarts that will deal a long-overdue mortal wound to this Beast we call Death.

JASPER: *(Still from bed, but no longer hiding under sheets.)* Why, Burt, is that *you* talking?! Are those words the altered creatures of your own tongue?

BURT: I implore you, exert your talent, in which now I place pure belief. Animate, by one act, both Ginger's life and my own boundless faith.

JASPER: I'd counted on you as a reliably disloyal detractor; now you switch roles on me. I'm confused, amazed, surprised, and—I fear—still unequal to the task that you, and Georgia before you, set for me to do.

BURT: *(Whimpering, supplicating, forsaking all pride.)* Only *try*, O miracle maker!

GEORGIA: *(To* JASPER, *like a fiery Joan of Arc.)* Try, damn you! I order you to try!

BURT: *(Like a wheedling puppy dog)* O glorious Might, try, I beg of you!

JASPER: *(Finally getting down from bed; but plainly terrified, a far cry from his calm saintlike serene confidence of before.)* All right, Burt, I'll do—or try to—what you mocked me for daring to think I could ever pull off before, though now *I* have the doubts about it that *you* once did. And you as well, Georgia, in your touching faith, or stern command, you prevail on me—to only try. Now in the crunch of my test, impotence devours me; and far from mastering Death, I feel my inadequacy before that fell master. In futility of faith and trembling void of grace, I'll go alas through my feeble motions. Weakly bending over Death's fresh new captive, I'll try to wrest her from the august dread of his awesome power.

(Kneeling, JASPER *extends his arms over* GINGER's *lifeless form. In absurd pantomime, he makes a pathetic, ridiculously half-hearted invocation, then pauses to test effect and result. In backfired melodrama turned flat, nothing whatever happens—* GINGER *remains still and lifeless. In a parody of grotesquely anguished failure,* JASPER *collapses in tears: witnessed by* GEORGIA *and* BURT, *who stand looking on, sagging in depression and despair.)*

(Cameo frozen tableau of above, all paused.)

(A moment later, GINGER's *eyes open. She stirs, then slowly comes to her feet. The three stare at her with amazement—and awe. It appears as though—after all— Jasper has miraculously derived powers from a majestic divine mystery.)*

GEORGIA: *(Elated and vindicated; to* BURT.*)* You see, you old Doubting Thomas—didn't I make a perfect choice in dropping you, on a wise spiritual impulse, in favor of my newer, truer love, the immaculate Saint of Death-Negation? He's done it!

BURT: But not till I, at the last minute, recanted my persistent skepticism, and prodded him with my belated faith, becoming most likely the critical key contributing factor in boosting him to the breakthrough marvel we have just witnessed: in all of history probably the one greatest single event to date; and *I (Pointing to himself in gloating pride.)* helped make it happen! Give me, then, a major credit!

GEORGIA: As though that would reverse my decision to make the switch of you for my noble Jasper! But aren't we being petty, in the wake of Death's glorious defeat? Let's lift up our acclaiming voice, as apostles in attendance to attest to this stirring occasion, this pure miracle. Simply to stand back in awe—not to quibble, but to quiver to cosmic vibrations—

GINGER: *(Dramatically cutting in on* GEORGIA; *suddenly beginning a harsh, mocking laugh.)* Ha! You fools! *(Pause, for stunned effect on other three.)* Merely playing possum, I was never the least bit dead whatever—just stunned somewhat. When Georgia held her mirror to my mouth, I made a quick decision: to hold my breath in under suspension, in order to discover, if each of you and all together thought me dead, what foolishness you'd be capable of. Thanks to my little impromptu ruse, this scientific deception of mine has revealed each of you most strangely. *(Pause. Turning to—on—*JASPER, *upbraidingly.)* As for you: When the chips were down, when under fire, when the call for courage was stressed squarely on the line, you let down your ideals ignobly, as your high principles cracked at the bend of the breaking point. Such weakness shows you even more despicable than when you earlier put on a holy mission and a saintly pretense. How vindicated I am for deciding to leave your bed and love, and break up with you after years I now regret! *(Contemptuously)* Enough, though, for you: why waste further words, in empty fury's lost song of bitterness, showing only how well I can scold and scorn? *(Turning now, abruptly, to* BURT.) As for *you*, weird turncoat of a Burt: I made the mistake of weaving a fancy full of love for you while Jasper described your reasonable realistic rejection of his request for faith in his abortive messiah crusade. Resolving on the spot to dispose of that deluded visionary, to replace him with sensible-seeming you on my love's aching throne, I was just about to leave this stale old bedroom and go seek you out and claim your rational aid in starting life and love all over, under an authentic sanctity of sanity. So then, by playing possum and feigning the ominous chill and lull of death, what have I discovered in *you*, the paragon of the down-to-earth, on which trait I placed love's value? Losing nerve in the test and crisis of crucial artificial stress, you beg like a dog, like a broken-down dog, for the very Miracle I'd credited you to discredit in the strong light of your skepticism. My admiration, love, respect for you have quickly, in the light of my springing this test on you, soured. My contempt for my outrageous discarded former love Jasper has now been shifted for even better reason to *you*. Thus, my opinion races to these unsound events, acutely critical of two loves in uncanny succession. The trick showed that, of all three of you, Georgia alone kept faith with her proclaimed point of view, sticking in crisis to her recently declared stance; though I deem her professed vision ill-conceived, glaringly defective, at least, in my mock contrived emergency, she forged decisive courage to uphold it, and alone acted out her misguided assumed role.

GEORGIA: *(To* GINGER*)* Thank you for your somewhat qualified compliment, and longwinded assurance that such a slimy thing as yourself dares compete with us to draw air again. *(Angrily)* How *dare* you scare us all to death by feigning a ploy of death, which drove me to such heights of unnecessary guilt!? Too cruel to be a practical joke—or scientific experiment, as you slyly justify it.

GINGER: *(Angrily)* It was a *fair* ruse, to call your bluff! How dare you—who nearly almost killed me—get on your high horse and scorn me so critical! What hardskinned nerve you have!

GEORGIA: *(Angrily)* The nerve you have, to say that *I* have nerve! *You* caused Jasper to act a mockery of his capabilities, to the undermining of his heroic credibility. In further unkindness, you even forced Burt into self-betrayal of his shallow, cool, skeptical creed! You deserve him! It was a detestably cynical thing to do!

GINGER: *(Angrily)* Was it, you violent ass? You nearly killed me—in earnest!

GEORGIA: *(Angrily)* Your death-feigning deception was even more earnest. Had you actually been completely and sincerely dead, Jasper would very well have performed the old Lazarus stunt on you, and raised you back to life's plateau from death's abysmal valley level. To resurrect Justice from the crooked, untrue test you rigged, I strike from the record what invalidly you brought to be. *(With threatening gesture)* And you yourself, I'd strike from the record—most willingly.

GINGER: *(With fury)* You nearly did—already. Let *me*, in kind, pay you back, to quite requite your nasty deed, by my bitter aping of your violence upon me! *(While saying that, she's swung her bag at* GEORGIA, *in vicious roundhouse, and clunked her full-blast on head, knocking* GEORGIA *instantly down, in her turn, into a death-resembling heap—but (audience is made to wonder) in earnest this time?)*

GINGER: *(To* JASPER, *vindictively)* There! You wanted somebody to resurrect; well, then, I *give* you somebody to resurrect!

JASPER: *(Appalled)* Could you have done that?! Why didn't you turn the other cheek?!

GINGER: *(Unrepentently)* I only repaid what I *owed* to Georgia; there, I've now discharged my one outstanding debt! *(Viciously)* Tauntingly, Jasper, I challenge you to prove yourself. You had your one chance before, which you proceeded comically or pathetically to bungle. I took matters into my own hands, to afford you another opportunity. Let's see what you can do *now*! Put your faith to action. I've tossed up the perfect test for it!

JASPER: Yes, but . . . but . . .

BURT: *(To* GINGER, *with admiration)* Oh Ginger, you're devastatingly superrational, after having proved yourself a woman of immense practical action. In swift succession, you've annihilated both of those sad and sloppy romantics, besides restoring me to my wholesome former state. I admire you almost to idol-worship, for what you've done, for what you've said! How well we go together, you and I! We're each other's logical mates by obviously natural selection from the jungle warfare of all these preceding events; we alone survive as sane! We're the superior lords of those *(Indicating* JASPER *and fallen* GEORGIA) fallen to the stupidity of their absurd faiths!

GINGER: *(Snuggling close to* BURT*)* Oh Burt, how wisely you analyze! Your love completes my queenly violence.

BURT: *(Snuggling close to* GINGER*)* Do let's sit side by side, spectators to the next sporting event: Jasper's attempt to revive his fallen new love. What shall we wager, on his success or otherwise? I offer you odds of ten to one he won't.

JASPER: *(Indicating* GEORGIA's *"corpse".)* Are you playful at a time like this!? How can you . . .

GINGER: *(To* BURT*)* A mere ten to one you offer me?! My dear Burt, the weakness and benevolence of your generosity, in the soft compassion of your mercy, still tarnish somewhat the staunch sanity of your cynicism. *(Viciously)* If realism were the true pure goal of yours, you'd offer me a *million* to one!

BURT: *(Converted into* GINGER's *spirit of things.)* Would I be *more* realistic, by offering a *zillion* to one?

GINGER: Not even! Just give me infinity-to-nothing! Those are the *likeliest* odds, in the weighed estimate of the plausible.

JASPER: *(His resolve returning)* Halt! you callously inhuman, viciously heartless pair of brain machines! Mock me together! But I'm your one hope, and one alone, to save you *(Glaring at* GINGER*)*, venomous Ginger, from the murderous consequences of your chilling violence, your "rational" retribution. *(To them both)* Set your playful odds at the grim mathematical wager to an absurd ratio: Bet your mightiest against me, you pair of calculating computers that ill conceal your insect souls: Offend me at your worst—heaping insult on insolence—the more will my success utterly upset your joint contempt!

BURT: *(Smugly, to* GINGER*)* Is he serious?—or crazed?

GINGER: He's both!

JASPER: I'll outreason you both, at your own idle game! *(To* GINGER, *in concession)* In *your* case, my former Ginger, you're right, it's true, I

proved pathetically inadequate to my self-imposed task of wresting you
from Death—though, in my defense, you were, of course, quite alive all
the time; nevertheless, my performance stunk out the joint—it was awful, it was a bomb. Now, to redeem and vindicate that miserable, ap-
palling fiasco, I'm determined, this time *(Looking down at* GEORGIA'*s*
lifeless-looking form), to challenge, head-on, one on one, my grim nemesis
Death, in direct man-to-man (if Death is a man) strife and clash—to the
finish! May the better man (if he's a man) win! To the victor belongs—
now that Georgia has thrown her lot on *my* side, having left Burt for
me—the spoils! I fling down my gauntlet *(Mimes this)* and issue mortal
defiance to the Grim One!

(As BURT *and* GINGER *watch,* JASPER *goes through his magic-invoking ritual again
but in complete contrast to the ineffectual, bungling effort before over* GINGER'*s
fallen body. This time, his incantation is mightily, majestically acted out—so much
so, that* BURT *and* GINGER, *as audience, applaud enthusiastically, like wild, delirious
spectators.)*

(In spite of this, the fallen GEORGIA *remains inert, unstirring.)*

BURT: *(Cuttingly)* Up to your old tricks, Jasper? You looked great, this
time. You were magnificent! What a performance! It brought down the
house—but it didn't bring up Georgia. But perhaps I quibble, over a
mere technical detail.

GINGER: *(Beaming on* BURT*)* Burt, how exquisitely cynical of you! You're
reconstituted now! An urbane model of supremely deft, cutting realism
annihilating those caught up in cloudy poetic magic! You show how
disbelief stands higher than the puffery of faith! I'm won over! You're
adorable!

*(*JASPER *is devastated, stung, by* BURT'*s remark.)*

*(*GINGER, *overcome once again with attraction to her new preferred man, kisses*
BURT *impulsively.* BURT *seizes the occasion to join in on the impulsive kiss—which
lingers, on and on, as they both, having thrown themselves into it, find it an
invigorating diversion—as* JASPER'*s rousing magic ritual performance was—from*
GEORGIA'*s fallen state, from which they seek the blessings of amorous oblivion.)*

*(Ignoring the twittering love-birds, and overcoming his having been stung and
devastated by* BURT'*s crack,* JASPER *goes back to work, with redoubled determination
and impressive, masterful-seeming concentration, over* GEORGIA'*s lifeless form
trying still another method of magical incantation.)*

(However, that doesn't have any effect, either. GEORGIA *is still unstirring. But this
time,* JASPER'*s effort, though definitely authoritative and impressive, was greeted
with no applause by* BURT *and* GINGER. *Nor is there another cutting, sarcastic
remark by* BURT.*)*

*(*BURT *and* GINGER'*s attention is mainly on each other, as they go on lying on the
bed, necking and petting, as though discovering each other as the right types for
each other through fleshly exploration, amorous touch and feel.)*

(JASPER pauses momentarily before resuming his enormous task, as though wondering what other method to try. BURT and GINGER take time out from their hugging, embracing, kissing, to notice that JASPER—though maintaining his dignity—is at a loss.)

BURT: *(To JASPER, in spirit of helpful cooperation rather than skeptical sarcasm.)* Jasper, may I suggest something? Since Ginger and I *(They keep fondling each other, etc., in illustration)* find kissing so very *invigorating*, perhaps *Georgia* might find it enough so to stir and revive from her dull, death-twinned stupor: were you to try that natural old formula, that homeopathic remedy of nature's simple erotics, that amorous resuscitation device—the kiss.

JASPER: If it invigorates you two *(Indicating BURT and GINGER's resuming, or rekindling, or redoubling, their panting embrace.)* to such shameless abandon and a display to delight even the most demanding voyeur, then perhaps the kiss technique might— *(Hopefully)* it just might—invigorate Georgia *(Looking down at her.)* here, to life's minimum display of breath. Just *breathing*, is all *I* exact. *(Primly, puritanically)* Not the *panting* condition of *you* shameless two *(Looking disapprovingly at them.)* but only, in Georgia's case, the modest, prim, unromantic little functioning of her lungs—physical yes, passionate no. That's all I require.

BURT: *(Losing patience)* Go ahead then—you can only try.

JASPER: *(Ignoring BURT; grandly, but ponderingly; theoretical, head in clouds.)* A kiss is the gateway to love. Perhaps love has the power to ignite, stir up, quicken, the momentarily inactive life. *(Looking at GEORGIA's fallen, lifeless form; rousing himself to the task.)* There she lies. I must try it. She's locked inside Death's grim house. Surely, Love must be the ultimate key—perhaps the skeleton key—to Life's lock, tampered with by Death's locksmith. With the kissful key of my lips, I'll pry open the misfunctioning difficulty—this deadlock of Death's lock.

(Getting on his hands and knees, JASPER demonstratively, flamboyantly, theatrically, but devoutly, plants a profound, prolonged kiss on GEORGIA's lifeless face. BURT and GINGER suspend their mutual fondlings to look on, rapt, while suspense builds up. JASPER persists—kissing with all his heart and soul.)

(At length—slowly—it works!)

JASPER: *(Still on hands and knees, leaning over the reviving GEORGIA.)* Were you in *Death*? Did I bring you back from it?

GEORGIA: Having been unconscious and oblivious at the time, I can't tell. If I *was* in Death—maybe I was—I bring back no report, nor finding, nor information, as to that dread state.

As to whether *you* brought me back from it: Not knowing whether I was dead or not, I don't know whether *you* brought me back—*if* I was *there*.

One thing, though: Waking up to your kiss was terribly nice. Even though I'm revived, can you repeat the dose?

JASPER: Most gladly. Not only did it do *you* good—*I* didn't mind it, either. Here goes.

(Still on hands and knees, JASPER leans over the still reclining GEORGIA, to repeat his long-drawn-out kiss ministration. From bed where they've been necking, BURT and GINGER also close-to in a kiss-clinch. Thus, the two new couples are seen simultaneously overlapping in full-blown new amorous discovering, dead set on roads to new intimacies through gradual stages that audience can observe.)

(Finally, the two couples end this phase of their kissings.)

GEORGIA: Jasper, I've regained enough strength to tell you that I'm determined to join and help your crusade to rid our old Earth—finally, forever—of that thing you may or may not have just brought me back from.

JASPER: Welcome aboard, my new love. Love is fun, while Death isn't. We sure know our priorities.

GEORGIA: Yes, we know what to value—and what's rotten, thus to be eliminated.

JASPER: We're a spiritual pair—together!

GEORGIA: By your side I take unflinching, steadfast stand, to help ready not *one* person's (such as, perhaps, my own) recovery, but the universal barrier-hurdling of our total species, the race itself.

JASPER: *(Relieved, then gradually taking charge.)* Finally, I have an ally! Burt and Ginger both refused, but Georgia's my true champion to step forth and rally me from self-doubt. *(To BURT)* To join me, Burt, she's left you: it's a just step. *(To GEORGIA)* We've unlumbered ourselves—or been unlumbered—of loves abruptly grown incompatible. As for those two *(Indicating BURT and GINGER)*, they deserve each other—it's a fitting match of two cold over-reasonings who'll take tepid comfort in each other.

(BURT and GINGER kiss passionately.)

JASPER: *(To GEORGIA)* As for *us*, we're a pair of passionates that blazingly merge to the same spiritual core. *(JASPER and GEORGIA kiss primly.)*

(To all three) Love has suffered today, but grown improved, in the radical surgery of the switches.

BURT: I wholeheartedly agree.

GEORGIA: I agree with all my heart.

GINGER: With my whole heart, I agree.

JASPER: Are we then all agreed?

BURT: Yes!

GEORGIA: Absolutely!

GINGER: Emphatically!

BURT: Then we seem at last to be positively in accord—all four of us, without exception. Might I safely make bold to venture such conclusion in the fullness of your endorsement?

GEORGIA: Yes!

GINGER: Absolutely!

JASPER: Emphatically!

GEORGIA: Our enthusiasm, then, seems to be positive, as well as unanimous. In that, are we in full accord?

GINGER: Yes!

JASPER: Absolutely!

BURT: Emphatically!

GINGER: *(Matter of factly)* Your affirmations are most reassuring. Well, I guess *that* settles *that*. Would you, perhaps, agree?

JASPER: Yes!

BURT: Absolutely!

GEORGIA: Emphatically!

JASPER: Well, that's that.
    From pain to joy, we've exchanged our way into new-fledged hearts. *(To* GEORGIA*)* Darling—finally I realize—it should *always* have been you! *(Pause. Reconsiders; changes mind. Now addresses all three.)* But maybe it's better *this* way—to be "born again," or to be "twice-born," or to be "reborn." *(To* BURT*)* Wouldn't you say so, Burt?

BURT: Yes it is! There's a new surge of energy, a new charge of excitement, by belated conversion! *(To* JASPER*)* No hard feelings, I hope, about my absconding with your recently phony-dead but genuinely self-resurrected Ginger, who's ditched your love most wisely to favor me instead?

JASPER: No hard feelings whatever, old man. You're entirely welcome to my former Ginger: make yourself free with her, to your double hearts' content. *(To* GINGER*)* But Ginger: if, perchance, you manage to retain luxury to sentimental emotions in your new regime of rational practicality, I do hope, in reflecting back occasionally on me in nostalgic remnants of your heart, you'll spot the ever-warm embers to set you missing me somewhat slightly a bit?

GINGER: Perhaps undoubtedly I surely might. How long ago already it seems! Yet we ended just tonight!

JASPER: Strangely, so it did.

GINGER: We'll feel just a wee bit contrite. For old times' sake. We'll rake a few regretful coals, stirring embers of remembrance in being members of the remnants of each other. But *you* weep—not I.

BURT: *(To* GEORGIA*)* You've left me. May you not regret it!

GEORGIA: *(In deliberateness, emphasizing sentence-ending rhymes)* We're both better off, my old dear. For old times' sake, we'll shed perhaps a tear. Tonight ended our many-a-year. A farewell kiss, old dear. *(They kiss.)*

GINGER: *(To* GEORGIA*)* We've traded *men*: For the better: *Amen.*

GEORGIA: I echo your very words. We've chosen fates more suited to our souls' respective bents. In choosing those fates for *ourselves*, we've been the active instruments for our men's accepting new fates which *we*, by pleasing *ourselves*, have bestowed on them. They've been controlled, by us!

GINGER: Shake, partner. *(They shake hands.)*

GEORGIA: And I have a promise to make.

GINGER: What?

GEORGIA: I'll never murder you again.

GINGER: I'll hold you to that. And *you* hold me to *this*: I vow never again to murder, even in retaliation, you as well! Embracingly, we seal this pact. *(They embrace, while* GINGER *continues.)* On this treaty of ours may well depend the stability and endurance of our freshly established love relations.

But do you suppose for an instant, that either Georgia or I—who are paragons of constancy and fidelity—have either forgotten or forgiven your unforgivable whimperings, simperings, and belief-reversals at my feigned death?

GEORGIA: How too true, my mutual understander. Will either of you survive such shame?

BURT: Ginger, may I vindicate myself? Your possum-playing test showed us two men failing in reverse ways: Jasper by lapsing from faith, and me by lapsing into faith. My embarrassed apology for my weakness goes thus: It was a momentary aberration at a time of stress, shock, alarm, fear, confusion, and concern for you, compassion for your state, longing to see you well again.

More recently, on the contrary, during my former Georgia's quite seeming death, inflicted so briskly by you—did not my reactions then atone admirably for such shortcomings and malperforming I fell prey to at earlier your own demise?

GINGER: Your critical capacity does *seem* restored, noble Burt; and the skeptic's scalpel may be sharpened to a surgical venom. *(Pause, in transition from praise to caution.)* But a word of caution: The weakness of your former lapse into flabby romantic faith still threatens dangers of recurrence. A ruthless vigilance, I now prescribe. You—demoted to a novice now in penalty of your shameful sentimental display—must take a solemn vow to undergo a disciplinary regimen of stern demands that I—in the role of trainer and coach—shall impose on you in ruthless rigor: a hardening program by which you shall regain an identity wholeness, a pure embodiment of the cynical principles of tough-minded superrational practical materialism. I'll crack the whip to enforce this reinforced development of your old self.

BURT: *(Down on his knees.)* Princess of Realism, Empress of Reason, Queen of the Worldly Realm, resigned to accept our mortal fate allowing no dream of hope: as I extol you I vow to perform and obey as your command sets forth, to rebecome fully what I was, and nevermore slip or disappoint.

GINGER: You may rise now. *(*BURT *rises)* Let's leave those two *(Indicating* JASPER *and* GEORGIA.*)* soft-minded saps. Their company sets the worst example. *(Bearing suitcase, packed with her clothes, etc. in one hand, and arm in arm with* BURT *with her other hand, she's leaving apartment with him.)* Of course, dear *(Indicating* JASPER *and* GEORGIA.*),* we *do* wish them well.

(They exit. JASPER *and* GEORGIA *are left to each other.)*

JASPER: A touching demonstration! Now that *they*'ve outlined the plain agenda for the ideological working of their love—what about you and me, Georgia? On what contrary ideology shall be based the structure of *our* working love?

GEORGIA: *(Undressing for bed, carelessly tossing her clothes around the room, in contrast to her previous, more repressed, stiff, or formal bedroom behavior with* BURT.*)* Ginger has extracted from Burt a solemn vow. From you, Jasper, I must extract a vow similarly solemn, though of opposite nature and reverse character. Ginger's possum-playing ploy demonstrated your weakness under stress. However sterling, stirring and—bravo—well done your perhaps resuscitation of myself may just have been, you earlier displayed a vulnerability that must be corrected. To that end, I now impose on you a stiff, severe regimen, a program of disciplinary demands designed to develop you into the pure embodiment of steadfast visionary zeal tempered to the perfect pitch that burns a blazing path through Death's smooth armor, hitherto unassailable.

I'll make you the right man for a tough job: one who'll tackle it head-on, and get the job done. When you get through, you will have wiped out the very dream we dreamed, the very vision we envisioned: you will have ruthlessly destroyed them the hard way—the unprecedented way: by replacing their *dream* and *vision* stuff, by stamping it all as now—behold *(Pause for effect.)* —Real!

JASPER: *(Down on his knees, just as* BURT *had just been in taking his vow to* GINGER.*)* Princess of Idealism, Empress of Vision, Queen of the passionate dream: As I extol you I vow to perform and obey as your command sets forth, to rebecome fully what I was, and nevermore slip or disappoint.

(As JASPER *is making that vow, lights come up on other (right) side of stage, on* BURT's *and* GINGER's *bedroom, where* BURT *and* GINGER *are getting into bed.)*

(Both couples kiss and turn out their respective lights at same time. Then sounds of ardent lovemaking are heard.)

(Continued darkness. End of scene.)

Scene Seven

(Stageset: Two separate bedrooms (in two separate houses, of course), revealed on opposite sides of stage: JASPER *and* GEORGIA *sitting up on their bed on the left;* BURT *and* GINGER *sitting up on their bed on the right. The years have abundantly gone by; all four characters are shown (aided by makeup, etc.) to have perceptibly and profoundly aged.)*

(On the left, JASPER *and* GEORGIA *are staring into the space in front of their bed. On the right,* BURT *and* GINGER *are reading books in their bed.)*

(Focus is on GEORGIA's *and* JASPER's *bedroom.)*

GEORGIA: When will it be? It should be before we're too old.

JASPER: It'll come! It'll come!

(Pause)

GEORGIA: Hurry! We're getting old!

JASPER: Death's end comes of its own accord. By voluntary will, I'm powerless to hasten it.

(Pause)

GEORGIA: Our love mustn't go the dwindling way of our flesh. Spare us! *Meet* this Death, and slay him!

JASPER: *(Irritated, admonishing)* For that, grant me peace.

(Pause. From this point on, the lights grow gradually dimmer and dimmer until, by the end of this final scene, there's total and final blackness to end the play.)

GEORGIA: *(Puzzled, in growing alarm)* Jasper—what's happening?

JASPER: Although I'm not sure, it could be that this might very well be it.

GEORGIA: "It"? What "it"?

JASPER: I'm referring, my darling, to my long, long-awaited encounter with my long-sought-out, mystically hand-picked adversary.

GEORGIA: *(Anxiously)* The approaching showdown becomes momentously imminent, momentarily eminent, ferociously at hand! At last, about to take place, is that meeting so counted on, planned for, deliberated on, in studied readiness and ever-steadied nerve. Are you at your fully prepared strength to cope head-on, on this collision course? Oh Jasper, my dear belovéd!

JASPER: *(Calm, tranquil, unperturbed) (Examining* GEORGIA *closely, with concern.)* You're agitated, you tremble. Is your longstanding equanimity, ever so faithful and confident, crumbling somewhat now with the onslaught of the dread unknown darkness?

GEORGIA: So it sadly seems. Whereas you, sterling Jasper, on the other hand are now become perfect in calm anticipation of what shall be triumphantly your *un*fatal encounter. How I remember...

JASPER: Remember what, my dear?

GEORGIA: Your brave calm spirit and ready magic holiness show such stark, decisive contrast to a scene so many years ago that the earlier scene seems placed already in an entirely previous lifetime!

JASPER: At such a time as this, are you referring to—?

GEORGIA: *(Fallen into a momentary trance of memory.)* I am...I can see it in a phantom of returned presence. Subjected suddenly to Ginger's possum-playing test, how inadequate you proved!: fumbling, incompetent, pathetic, an impromptu revelation of such total, pitiful lack in the very confidence and faith which— *(Recovering from trance, looking up at* JASPER.*)* —now...

JASPER: —Which now, in almost excessive abundance, I do have? I owe my recovery and reformed development to you. For it was your own perhaps lifeless form on which my first perhaps struggle against Death took perhaps place. Then, on vowing knees at your recovered feet, I swore on sacred oath such firmness—

GEORGIA: *(Interrupting)* But now look at *me—I* tremble! This time it's no toy trial or mock test. It all stares at us; it's *for real!*

JASPER: My darling, I feel that too. There *is* something real; it's coming on a-nigh. It's breathing on us.

My old vow—. All my life since has been slow preparation, arduous, uphill, towards this very strangeness, this event obscured in the vastness of its own uncertainty, which now, in glorious suspension or eerie suspense, hangs pending, impending, nigh, already here—upon us—at hand—closely knotted in the tissue of our breathing, at one with us, permeable with us ...

GEORGIA: *(Uneasy; somewhat whiningly)* You're honed, primed, steeled, for it; you're raised to its level (whatever "it" may be); but not *me*— I'm jittery!

JASPER: *(August, calm, imperious)* Stop gnashing about. Calm yourself.

GEORGIA: *(Shrill, uneasy)* Advice is cheap. *(Pause)* Kiss me. *(*JASPER *kisses her.) This* time, your kissing hasn't done the trick of when you first tried it on me. Did your first kissing revive me, save me? Where's the magic *this* time? I'm too far gone now, the tides have overtaken me, I'm past the grace of recovery, beyond the blissful benefit?

JASPER: This time, is not the past. Calm yourself. We're coming on a greater unknown.

GEORGIA: *(Shrieks)* But what's your formula?!

(Focus now shifts to other side of stage, other bedroom: GINGER *and* BURT *sitting up reading in bed.)*

GINGER: Burt, something's wrong with this light! Have you noticed it?

BURT: Indeed. I must confess that, by all appearances, it's getting more difficult to read. Please do this favor—check the light switch. The realistic, practical, down-to-earth step for us to make would be to locate the difficulty, by getting empirically to the concrete root of this mechanical illumination problem, to make simplicity of its complication, and sensibly to fix it. I recommend this simple course of action, as directly bearing on, and alleviating, our complaint that the light seems to wane.

*(*GINGER *does as requested, checking the light switch.)*

GINGER: My dear longstanding partner of domesticity, Burt: When it comes down to it (though I'm not a licensed electrician, nor even an amateur specialist), there appears nothing whatever to be wrong with the light switch, so far as what its *surface* would indicate, beyond which my normal vision can't penetrate, especially in *this* dwindling light. In short, I report: I'm in the dark.

BURT: Then, could there be something wrong with the lamp? Logically, you should examine that next. Obviously, this increasing dimness must be traced to its correct causality.

*(*GINGER *goes to examine lamp, then reports back.)*

GINGER: I've discovered nothing mechanically amiss with this lamp, within the capacity of what I'm able to determine. *(Pause)* Burt! I fear— *(Hesitates)*

BURT: Fear!? Fear what?

GINGER: *(Timid at first, then gradually more out of control in disobedience to* BURT.*)* That—I venture to conjecture—it's not electrical problems that we're facing. That there's "something else": something even too specific for words. *(Agitated)* To me, it all looks too fishy, or creepy, or ... There's something grim or gruesome going on. I dread to even *imagine* what it must come out to be. *(Now in terror.)* Burt! My terror is worried over it! I'm sick where my body can never reach!

BURT: *(Reprimandingly)* You're letting me down! Your silly phobia about some apparently engulfing darkness contrasts shockingly with that memorable occasion of long ago: Playing a brilliant pose of possum, you evinced such superior practical supremacy to the rest of us who failed in ignominy and fell apart in odd assorted heaps of imbecility.

Then, you astounded further, having in perfection of retribution ostensibly slain Georgia my former love, when above her fallen remnants you laughed at apparent death's gruesome trappings by kissing me in passionate abandon.

Then it was I took my stern vow of resolve to be your disciple, to harden myself, steel-like, to a spartan regime of realism and a bone-dry devotion to the rational.

I implore you: rally yourself! After years of dishing it out, practice those precepts that *I*, in arduous obedience to the rigors of your discipline, have now contemptuously mastered!

GINGER: I'm compelled, Burt, in my gathering fear, to disobey. I must persist, then, in insisting: The problem we both face is strictly non-electrical, in a non-appliance sense. I dread to intuit—yet intuit I must—that there's "something else" afoot. For the life of me, I can't put my imaginative finger on it; yet it stares me brazen in the face. What it can be, I wouldn't want to look in the face. *(Terrified)* Burt—hold me, I'm scared!

*(*BURT *obeys, holds her, but perfunctorily, with no passion or conviction.)*

GINGER: Kiss me! I need love!

*(*BURT *obeys, kisses her, but perfunctorily.)*

BURT: Ginger—

GINGER: *(Eagerly; starving for some love affirmation, a sign of passion.)* Yes!? Yes!?

BURT: *(Coolly)* Do reach into the side table drawer, and pull out the electrical repair manual, won't you? *(Sees her do this. Coldly.)* The next step, of course, is to hand it over to me. *(She does so. Then, with chilling formality.)* That's terribly kind.

(Squinting in the ever-dimming light to read repair manual, BURT *leaves* GINGER *alone with her mounting fear, her chilled loneliness, her love deprivation.)*

(Focus shifts back to the left, to other bedroom.)

JASPER: *(Slowly, gravely)* Across great Darkness, encountering terrors that belong only to the Unknown, double-mounted on one slow steed of Love, we travel in quest of timelessness. Suspend your breath. Stop your heart. We're not in this bedroom. We're lost, directionless, and hand in our senses, abandon them. . . .

GEORGIA: *(Alarmed)* It should be the *other* way: brighter! more vivid!

JASPER: *(In comparison with* GEORGIA—*gravely, slowly, wonderingly, discoveringly.)* Hush up your interference! Ordinary expectations don't apply here. Stop preparing. Abandon habitual logic. We're in a world-lessness. It's beginning to envelop us. No more mental "meaning," now. We're coming into word-lessness.

GEORGIA: *(Half-shrieking)* I'll quit! I back out! Is there no will left?!

JASPER: *(Slow tempo, gravely)* Are we there? My final feeling is only familiar fear.

GEORGIA: Have you won? Or lost?

JASPER: It's *"we"*—in *either* case.

GEORGIA: *(Ordering)* Define our state!

JASPER: No definitions ease this complete change. It's beyond our figuring out. We're converted into sound-lessness. What *we* are . . . is only what we *were*. *(Pause)* Something we've never been without, is stopping: It's what we knew as . . . "Now."

(Focus switches back, in gradually further dwindling light, to right side of stage, to other bedroom.)

BURT: *(Straining and squinting in dim light; but calmly reading instructions out loud from repair manual.)* Detach the lampshade from its axis base. Lower the switch from its adjacent hook. Pluck out the plug from its companion socket. Check the bulb's metal filament magnet. Using plyers, carefully dismantle . . .

GINGER: *(Increasingly fearful while following* BURT's *instructions and dismantling lamp.)* It's not working—*nothing* is working!

BURT: *(Stops squinting at repair manual; turns to squint at* GINGER *instead; admonishingly.)* Resist hysteria; cling to rational practical realism at all odds, at any cost. We must determine what in this world—or to be more precise, in this *room*—is so irritatingly, disturbingly wrong, that we can't put it to rights. Everything—which includes anything— is explainable.

(Squints more at GINGER*)* You look, in the groping scarcity of light, troubled, disturbed, agitated, bothered; so I ask, multibly: What's your

fuss or disturbance? What's bothering you, or eating you? Woman, what's up?!

GINGER: *(Jitteringly agitated, but defiant)* There's more at foot, or wherever, or at hand, or wherever, than meets, dear Burt, the apparent eye of your speculation. Shallow mechanical facts won't help us now. *(Pause; alarmed, decisive)* We're in for it!

BURT: *(Scoffing)* Nonsensically pumped-up melodrama, richly thrilling! You indulge your sweet throb of delicious terror!

GINGER: *(Vehement)* I'm not in this for fun! This is no enjoyment feast! Neither pleasure nor delight attends my conviction: Something's lurking—more than meets the fading eye.

(Focus now includes both sides of stage, both bedrooms.)

JASPER: *(Now standing on bed, peering forward, thrust into unknown, like figurehead on prow of ship. Speaking with cadence of incantation.)* What we are—is only what we *were*. Something we've never been without, is stopping: It's what we knew as—"Now." *(Pause)* Just what was that "now"? (Strange to be almost looking back!) Now by now by now; it was the familiar succession, duration, sequence, consecutiveness, of now by now by now, like the common daily air of the ever-reassuring breath of atmosphere all around about us in the air of ever-onward consciousness. Now by now by now— *(Pause. In a stroke of grave fright-realization:)* But there's no "now," now! *(Shouting)* No more "now"! We've run out of "now"s!

BURT: *(Sitting on edge of bed, squintingly and strainingly referring to electrical handbook manual. Scolding GINGER.)* Don't you stall! In the socket mechanism are those wires fastened securely? Don't go lax! Brace up!

GEORGIA: *(Clutching a leg of JASPER, who's still standing on their bed.)* Am I deceived? Are you fraud—or are you saint? Which is it, finally? Reveal a conclusion! Am I unforgiving—or grateful? I insist I be told! This loyalty I invested . . . What returns on our faith? *(Slight pause)* How did we come out?

GINGER: As to what's happening *(Kneeling on floor beside bed)* —there's not only more than meets the eye, but the eye, in its turn, isn't met any more, it being too dark.

From the eye's side, and from the side of what feeds and meets the eye, there's equally the falling away. There's less than meets the eye, and less the eye itself—and even the "less" runs out.

Now, there's no eye: for there's nothing to meet it! *(Weeping with terror.)*

JASPER: In conclusion, what is there to conclude? I sought immortality for every member of my club here—the Humanity Club, that doesn't exclude anyone. But it seems we four have been admitted to a club of even broader membership, to the least exclusive club of all—to the club of nonexistence.

(To audience) Join us, there's no hurry. Join us, when, in common with us, you're unmade with the same lack of clay. Time shall unite us But don't make haste. Procrastinate. Joining us too soon would be self-destructive. Put it off.

CURTAIN